Using Feng Shui

EASY WAYS TO USE THE ANCIENT
CHINESE ART OF PLACEMENT FOR
HAPPINESS AND PROSPERITY

Using Feng Shui

EASY WAYS TO USE THE ANCIENT
CHINESE ART OF PLACEMENT FOR
HAPPINESS AND PROSPERITY

ANTONIA BEATTIE

CONSULTANT - ROSEMARY STEVENS

RAINCOAST BOOKS
Vancouver

Contents

happiness - *fu*

peace - *p'ing*

Introduction

The concept that there is a powerful form of energy flowing around your home and workplace which affects your life and well-being originated in a number of ancient civilizations, including China, many centuries ago. In China, it is believed that this energy is like the force of the wind ("feng") and the flow of water ("shui"). It is believed to be a living energy that can flow or stagnate according to the shape and form of your environment. If it flows at a gentle, steady pace, it brings benefits, such as good fortune and health. If it is allowed to stagnate, the energy may bring with it illness, unhappiness and poor luck. Like wind and water, this energy can be manipulated to flow beneficially and this is part of the art of feng shui.

Not only does this energy, known as qi or chi, flow through our cosmos and earth but also through our own bodies. By rearranging the flow of the external energy, we can also dramatically change the flow of our internal energy. The practice of feng shui is based on the theory that there is a profound connection between human beings and nature. By understanding and tapping into the flow of life energy through nature, we can effectively link into nature's powerful balance and harmony.

Feng shui can ultimately give us the power to take control of our lives. It helps us transform our homes and places of business into efficient conductors of the universal energy. By doing this, we are inviting harmony into our lives.

This book has been designed to give you a simple introduction to the principles of feng shui, taking into account the practices of some of the more prominent schools of thought. Solutions, in the form of cures or remedies, to help activate the flow of energy or correct imbalances, will also be given, introducing you to a powerful tool to help alleviate recurring problems in your life.

If you feel that you are not getting ahead in your career or that you always seem to be involved in relationship or family tensions, turn to the chapter concerning your particular issue and find out how easy it can be to change your life and to find a new sense of balance and purpose.

energy - *ch'i*

What is Feng Shui?

In China, it is believed that there is a universal energy form, called qi (or chi), that flows through and around all life forms. There are three important levels of qi – heaven qi, earth qi and human qi.

Heaven qi includes planetary and weather-inducing qi and is energy that flows around the planets, clouds and wind. Earth qi can be forces that make up our natural landscape, such as mountains, the sea and magnetic fields, or human-made environmental structures, such as dams, shopping malls and residential buildings. Human qi is made up of social qi, such as the forces that flow between friends and family, and personal qi, such as the energy that moves through your body, thought processes and personality.

It is important for the different types of qi to flow gently, freely and without impediment. If energy is allowed to do this, particularly along gentle curves, this kind of beneficial qi is known as "sheng qi". If the qi is blocked or becomes stagnant, it turns into a negative form of energy called "sha qi". Sha qi can be created by long tunnels that encourage qi to move too fast and in straight lines. This concentrates the energy and it develops a strong, destructive force. Sha qi can also be created by sharp corners, both in terms of the shape of a room and of prominent pieces of furniture. This form of sha qi is known as "poison arrows".

This link between humankind, earth and heaven is the central focus of the Chinese philosophy of the Tao or "the way".

It is believed that what keeps qi moving on all three levels is the constant movement between two opposing forces — yin and yang (see pages 10–11). Earth qi is also aided by the five elements — earth, wood, fire, metal and water (see pages 12–13).

Energy at Your Doorstep

Qi can also pick up excess energy from a particular direction which can affect your home while it is passing through the building. The following illustration shows the type of energy your door will attract, according to the direction it is facing:

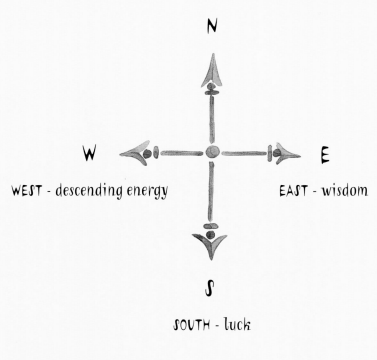

NORTH - nurture

N

W — WEST - descending energy

E — EAST - wisdom

S

SOUTH - luck

The feng shui philosophy seeks the balance between two universal opposing forces, yin and yang. These forces energize qi and affect every aspect of the universe. Once yin and yang are in balance, the life force is in balance, which leads to a sense of well-being and prosperity in your life.

Everything in the universe can be categorized as either yin or yang. The yin and yang symbol, where the black, symbolizing yin (female energy) and the white, symbolizing yang (male energy) swirl around each other, represents harmony in the universe. Although these forces are opposite, they are complementary to each other. As the yin and yang symbol indicates, each force contains a small amount of the other's energy.

In a building's interior, yin energy would be expressed through the use of dark colors, as well as the cool hues of green and blue. Yin is also the energy in empty spaces and around curved walls or screens. Yang energy can be expressed through bright, warmly colored walls and is the energy around the furniture in the room, as well as around straight walls. It is important that there is a balance between dark and bright colors in your rooms and between space and furniture.

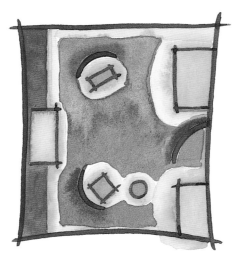

If your room is too yin — dark, damp and with very little furniture — there is likely to be too little vital energy in the room, which might make you feel lethargic and unrested. You will need to introduce more furniture and bright, rich colors to balance the room and give it more energy. If your room is too yang, that is bright, dry and cluttered with furniture, there will be too much vital energy, which might induce headaches, jumbled focus and accidents. You will need to take some furniture out of the room and include some dark or calming colors to balance the brightness.

Sometimes houses themselves may be too yin, particularly if they are near places of death, such as cemeteries, funeral homes or places where death is mourned, such as places of religious worship.

To counterbalance the yin atmosphere around your house, incorporate brightly colored features in your yard, perhaps a red fence, bench, front door or even roof.

If your home is too yang, for example, if you are near large factories or stadiums, you may wish to incorporate some water features around your house and paint your front door a cool, dark color.

In feng shui, a lucky house or room is one in which there is allowance for the proper flow of qi (see pages 8–9) which is accomplished by having a balance between yin and yang energies (see pages 10–11). Feng shui principles also state that there must be a productive link between the elements. The Chinese believe there are five elements or forces of nature that are in a constant state of movement — wood, fire, earth, metal and water. The different directions of the compass — north, south, east and west respectively — correspond with the elements water, fire, wood and metal whilst earth is considered the center of the compass. These elements also either have a positive or negative effect on each other.

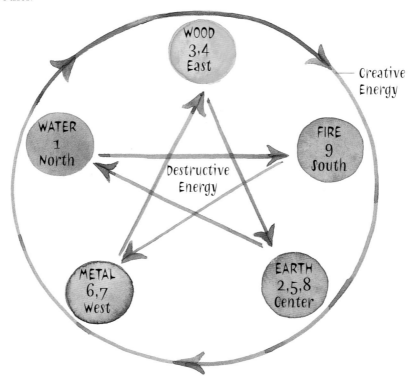

Consideration of the elements can help you identify whether the floor plan of your home or place of business is auspicious. Each room in a house usually has a purpose that can be ascribed to one of the elements, such as the kitchen to fire or the bathroom to water. Their position in your home will be auspicious if the direction of the room corresponds with the same or sympathetic element. For instance, in considering whether a kitchen is well positioned, remember that fire corresponds with the south direction while wood, which has a creative relationship with fire (see the diagram opposite), corresponds with the east direction. According to feng shui principles, a kitchen is auspiciously positioned if it faces the south, east or south-eastern direction.

It is believed that everything on earth, including human beings, are made up of a combination of the elements. However, each person's year of birth indicates which element is predominant in their personality.

Find your element

To find out which element is ascendant in that it represents your personality, make a note of the last digit of your year of birth. The following table outlines the dominant element for the Chinese solar years according to the end digit of each year. If your birthday falls in January or February, consult the table on pages 78–79 to check whether your birth date falls in the previous year in the Chinese system.

This table also indicates whether your personality is yin or yang (see pages 10–11), that is, introvert or extrovert. Other compatibility issues in feng shui are discussed on pages 58–59.

Last digit of year of birth	Element	Yin/Yang
1	Metal	Yin
2	Water	Yang
3	Water	Yin
4	Wood	Yang
5	Wood	Yin
6	Fire	Yang
7	Fire	Yin
8	Earth	Yang
9	Earth	Yin
0	Metal	Yang

Feng shui practitioners believe that not only are the elements linked to compass directions but so are the eight aspirations or enrichments of life. The table below lists the aspirations and their corresponding compass directions. The North system uses the traditional correspondences applied by the Chinese masters. The South system is used mainly by practitioners in the southern hemisphere, although there is still strong debate as to the validity of changing the directions, and it is generally not recommended. The table also lists the pages where the aspirations of life are discussed in further detail throughout the book:

Aspiration	North system (see pages 20–21)	South system (see pages 20–21)	Reference pages in this book
Wealth	Southeast	Northwest	48–51
Acknowledgment and fame	South	North	52–56
Relationships	Southwest	Northeast	56–59
Family and health	East	West	62–63, 70–71
Creativity and children	West	East	68–69
Knowledge	Northeast	Southwest	66–67
Career	North	South	64–65
Mentors and travel	Northwest	Southeast	60–61

In feng shui, the areas in your house corresponding with the compass directions must have a good flow of positive energy (see pages 8–9) and should maintain a balance of yin and yang features. Ideally, the function of the rooms should correspond auspiciously with the elements (see pages 12–13). However, if the rooms do not correspond, there are a number of remedies to help balance the energy (see pages 38–47).

Over four thousand years, a number of feng shui schools have evolved with different ideas as to which areas of the home or place of business correspond with each compass direction (see page 16). There are different approaches by those using a simple grid calculation based on the bagua (see pages 18–19), using compass directions with the bagua (see pages 20–21) or your east/west orientation (see pages 22–27). The rules of each approach are examined in this book.

The placement of a goldfish bowl in the wealth corner of a room can be a simple remedy for financial problems.

There are three schools of feng shui – bagua feng shui, compass feng shui and form feng shui. This book will concentrate on bagua feng shui, which involves applying a grid to your house or place of business. At its simplest, the grid can be based on the position of your front door (see pages 18–19). or you can work out how your house is positioned according to the elements and compass directions, by using the grid formation described on pages 20–21.

The compass school of feng shui concentrates on distinguishing between people and houses which fall into "east" and "west" categories (see pages 22–27). To understand the relationship between you and your house, you can determine whether your personal orientation suits the orientation of your house or place of business.

The compass school uses the "luo pan", a special feng shui compass which also contains a Western-style compass. Around the compass, in concentric circles, sometimes with up to 64 of them, the trigrams of the bagua, as well as the compass directions, elements and other information related to the trigrams can be read. A trigram is a stack of three broken or unbroken lines which have various associations. The luo pan shows the inter-relationship between these important features of feng shui.

The form school of feng shui concentrates on the flow of qi in the environment. It emphasises the importance of the shape of the environment around your house, the position of roads, rivers and mountains in relation to your house and the way these can affect the flow of qi to your front door (see pages 32–37).

Feng shui is not simply the rearrangement of furniture. It helps us to take control of our lives by making us appreciate the patterns of the world around us and how they reflect the patterns that are flowing within us.

There is no more immediate an indication of the state of our mind and body than the way we decorate our homes. Often a cluttered room may be an indication that we feel cluttered in our mind or lives. Throw out the unnecessary clutter in your home by prioritizing what the most important things to have in your house are. It is believed that by doing so you are triggering your mind to take the same action so that you make space for the more important things in your life, allowing you to focus clearly on finding success and fulfilment.

In feng shui terms, by clearing away the clutter, you are inviting a stronger life force (qi) to flow through your home, bringing with it clarity of thought. Specific areas of your life, such as your career (see pages 64–65), may be strengthened by uncluttering the corresponding areas of your home.

Applying Feng Shui

A SIMPLE GRID CALCULATION

One of the most important aspects of feng shui is working out which areas of your house correspond with which aspiration or enrichment: wealth, fame, relationships, health, creativity, knowledge, career and travel. There are a number of techniques, most of which can be expressed in the form of a three-by-three grid. This grid system, commonly referred to as the bagua, or pa-kwa (see pages 20–21) was derived from the luo-shu or magic square. The later Heaven sequence luo-shu square, which is the most frequently used, is said to have been derived from the markings on the back of a huge turtle. The shell was divided equally into nine squares, each square containing an arrangement of dots, from one to nine.

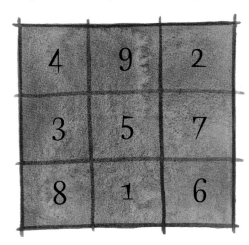

The use of the bagua grid system varies between feng shui schools. At its simplest, the grid is aligned according to the position of the front door, irrespective of compass directions. However, most feng shui practitioners use much more advanced methods, such as aligning the aspirations with the directions of the compass (see pages 20–21 for information about the bagua and pages 22–27 for information about your east–west orientation).

To begin your exploration of the principles of feng shui, try the simple grid formation first. As you become more familiar with these principles, try using the bagua with compass directions or exploring the possibilities of the east–west system. Use your intuition as to which system would best suit your house. Each system has validity and can show you how to increase the potential of your life.

To construct a simple grid formation, all you need to do is sketch it or find a plan of your house and draw a shape around your plan which will make it, if it is not already, a symmetrical square or rectangle. Do not worry about indentations or projections, such as porches or sundecks. On a separate piece of paper, draw a three-by-three box, dividing the symmetrical shape of your house into nine roughly equal sections.

Make a note of where your front door is situated. Your front door is the one which is most often used by your family and visitors. This may not be your formal front door. Copy the aspirations from the grid below, aligning the bottom of the grid (with the aspirations, from left to right, of Education, Career and Mentors) with the wall on your plan which contains your front door. You do not need to worry about compass directions with this system.

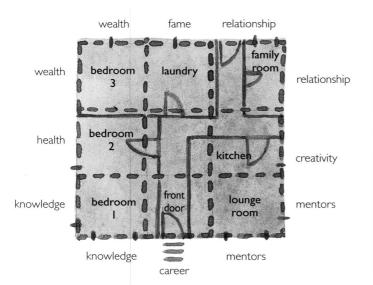

Feng Shui Tip

You will find that if your house is not symmetrical and there is a section missing in your plan, you may well be experiencing some difficulties in the corresponding aspiration of your life. Turn to the relevant pages discussing that particular aspiration, such as *Lovers, Mentors* and *Family* on pages 56–63, and learn how to balance and bring good fortune to that section of your home and life.

The bagua, or pa-kwa, is an octagonal picture or object that contains a trigram in each of its eight sides and an image of the yin/yang symbol in the center. A trigram is a picture of three lines stacked on top of each other. These lines are either broken or unbroken and their various combinations as trigrams represent certain aspirations or enrichments, such as wealth, fame, relationships, family and health, creativity, knowledge, career and helpful people (see pages 14–15).

Each side of the octagon also represents the eight compass directions, giving a corresponding direction to each aspiration or enrichment. The central image of the yin/yang symbol represents the element earth, as this is the basis of every home or place of business. See below the "former" Heaven Sequence, which is no longer used.

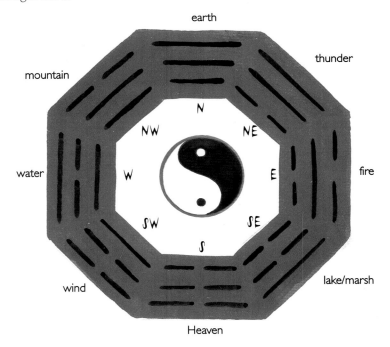

These eight trigrams are thought to be the forerunners to the 64 trigrams used in the I-Ching or Book of Changes. The I-Ching is a poetic means of divination devised over 3,000 years ago. With the development of the I-Ching, the sequence of the trigrams was altered, dividing feng shui practitioners into two camps: those who used the "former Heaven sequence" (see previous page) and those who used the "later Heaven sequence" (below). The "later Heaven sequence" is the one most commonly used today for bagua readings.

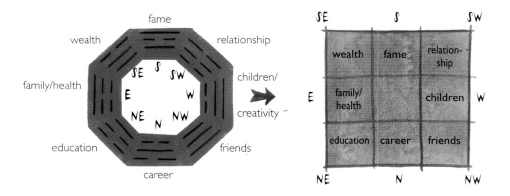

It has been argued that the "former Heaven sequence" was devised specifically for feng shui use, while the later sequence was devised for use with the I-Ching. However, some people believe that the former Heaven sequence does not relate to how life really is. Feng shui practitioners of both schools find their technique successful, so follow your intuition about which system you would like to use.

You will need to sketch or find a plan of your house and draw lines around your plan which will make it, a symmetrical square or rectangle, if it is not already. On a separate piece of paper, draw a three-by-three box, dividing the shape of your house into nine roughly equal sections. Copy the grid above and place the bottom of the grid (ie. Education, Career and Friends) along the northern wall of your house plan.

WHAT IS YOUR LUCKY DIRECTION?

Good fortune may be increased by placing your bed, desk or favorite chair so that it faces the direction favorable to you. Similarly, you can balance your unlucky directions with certain feng shui cures (see pages 38–47). The following calculations will help you work out your orientation and favorable directions. The feng shui system provides a choice between an eastern or western orientation.

First, add together the digits of the year of your birth. For example, if it is 1960, you should add $1 + 9 + 6 + 0$ to get a total of 16. Divide the total by 9, that is, 16 divided by 9, which gives you 1 with a remainder of 7. Now focus on the remainder, 7.

If you are male, subtract the remainder from 11, ie $11 - 7 = 4$. If you are female, add 4 to your remainder, ie $7 + 4 = 11$. As the resultant number is higher than 9, subtract 9 from the resultant number, ie $11 - 9 = 2$.

If you get 1, 3, 4 or 9, your orientation is east and the following directions are favorable:

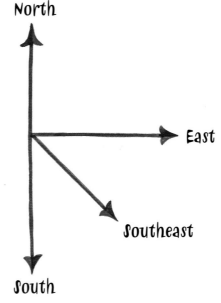

North

East

Southeast

South

It follows from our example that a man born in 1960 has an eastern orientation. He would experience a good flow of beneficial energy in his home if his front door was facing east. However, a woman born in 1960 has a western orientation. If a woman gets 2, 6, 7 or 8, her orientation is west and the following directions are favorable:

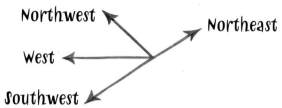

If you get zero with your calculation, chose 9 itself as your orientation number. If you get 5 as your orientation number and you are female, change your number to 8. If you are male and 5 is your orientation number, change your number to 2.

Be careful if your birthday falls at the beginning of the year. As we are using a Chinese system, it would be wise to use the Chinese solar calendar to see whether your year of birth number is really the previous year (see pages 78–79). For example, if you were born on 26 January 1960, your year of birth number is 59 because the Chinese year of 1959 ends on 28 January 1960.

Feng Shui Tip

You will find that if you sit at your desk or stand at your work station with your back facing any of your lucky directions, you can concentrate better and will be able to enhance your good fortune. If you place your bed in a position where your head is pointing in your lucky direction, you will find that you will be able to sleep more soundly and restfully.

Do the calculations on pages 22–23 to work out your personal orientation number and whether you are of an eastern or western orientation. You can also find out if your house has an eastern or western orientation. To feel relaxed and safe in your home, your house's orientation should ideally match your own. If you live in a house that has an opposite orientation to your own, you may experience arguments, illness, unhappiness in friendships and other relationships, as well as demotion in your career and accidents. However, there are ways of counterbalancing the energy flow (see pages 48–77).

The best way to work out your house's orientation is to determine its sitting direction. Find out which compass direction the back of your house is pointing towards; this is its sitting direction. In apartments, it is important to work out the sitting direction of the building that contains your apartment and the relationship of your apartment to the building. For instance, if the back of your apartment building faces north and the front door of your apartment faces the back of the building, your sitting position is still to the north, even though what you would think of as the front of your apartment is facing north.

If your building or house is sitting in the following compass directions, your home's orientation is to the east:

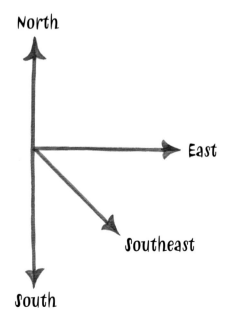

North

East

Southeast

South

If your building or house is sitting in the following compass directions, your home's orientation is to the west:

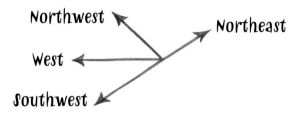

To work out your home's orientation by compass, stand with your back against the outside wall at the back of your house or building. Align your compass to the north and read the compass grade to work out which way the back of your house or building is facing. Use the table below to work out what your compass grade means:

Compass grade	Sitting direction
22.5 – 67.5	Northeast
67.5 – 112.5	East
112.5 – 157.5	Southeast
157.5 – 202.5	South
202.5 – 247.5	Southwest
247.5 – 292.5	West
292.2 – 337.5	Northwest
337.5 – 22.5	North

Your house or place of business has areas that are particularly lucky for you. It is important that you spend the majority of your time in your lucky areas. If you do not, you may feel uncomfortable in your house or workplace and experience demotion, unhappy relationships or accidents. You can also burglar-proof the windows and doors in unlucky areas, as they are more susceptible to break-ins. It is particularly important that your bedroom is in a lucky area so you have restful sleep and that your desk or any other area where you spend a lot of time is also in a lucky area, for maximum productivity.

To find out which areas in your house or place of business are lucky for you, take a separate piece of paper and trace the grid you made following the instructions on pages 20–21. You will not need to transfer the aspirations. To apply your favorable orientation to the grid of your home or place of business, you will need to refer again to the luo-shu square (see pages 20–21). Please note that you cannot use the simple grid method outlined on pages 18–19 for this exercise, as it does not take compass directions into account.

If you are of a western orientation, numbers 2, 6, 7 and 8 are favorable and relate respectively to the compass directions of southwest, northwest, west and northeast. On your grid, shade the following squares to indicate your lucky directions. The blue areas are your unlucky directions.

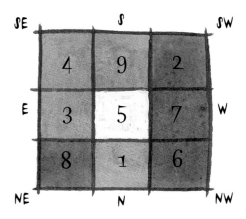

If you are of an eastern orientation, numbers 1, 3, 4 and 9 are favorable directions and relate respectively to the compass directions of north, east, southeast and south. On your grid, shade the following squares to indicate your lucky directions. The blue areas are unlucky directions.

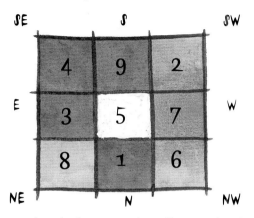

Calculate the lucky and unlucky areas for all your family members or colleagues. Find out the personal orientation of each person by using the system described on pages 22–23. If you are compatible with your premises and the other people are not, you can suggest changing their entrance into the building so it faces one of their favorable directions or change their bedrooms to rooms in their lucky areas. This will go a long way towards making your family or colleagues feel comfortable in areas where they spend a lot of time. Use your intuition or consult a professional feng shui practitioner for advice.

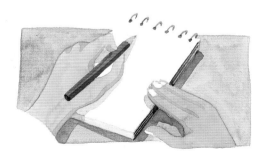

Your Home and its Effect on Your Life

THE SHAPE OF YOUR HOME

In feng shui, it is important that your house has balance and symmetry. Square or rectangular houses, in terms of the floor plan, are considered most conducive to the best flow of qi. The ideal shape for a plot of land is one that is also either square or rectangular. Triangles or other irregular plot shapes are the least auspicious.

The position of your house on your plot of land is also important. On a square plot of land, the best position is right in the center, while on a rectangular plot, the house is best positioned near the front of the land.

The form school of feng shui believes that the regular shape of a square or a rectangle does not create sharp angles that make it difficult for qi to flow in and out. This is a particular problem with a triangular plot of land. The inability of qi to flow freely leads to stagnation, which in turn leads to the creation of "poison

auspicious

auspicious

arrows" of negative energy which are detrimental to your health and luck. If your house is not a regular shape, you can cure this by placing features in your garden which extend the line of your house to make it symmetrical.

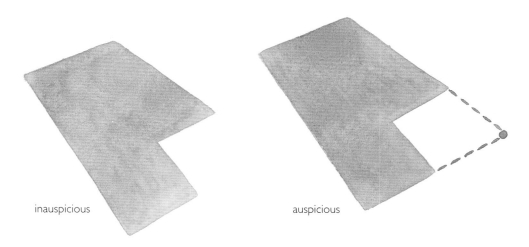

inauspicious   auspicious

Squares correspond with the earth element and a home of this shape gives its occupants a sense of stability and endurance. Rectangles correspond with the element of wood and are symbolic of growth and resilience. Shapes related to the elements of fire, water and metal are not as auspiciously formed to provide the occupants with the best flow of qi. The flow of qi in triangular houses, such as A-frame buildings, can be as unpredictable as fire, with the top of the triangle creating a great deal of sha qi. Circular houses, which are related to the element of metal, are believed to create too strong a swirl of energy, which can overwhelm its occupants and create headaches, lack of focus and poor sleep. Houses that correspond to the element of water always strike the observer as a jumbled mess of shapes, providing an up-and-down flow of qi which also causes an unstable sensation.

A horseshoe-shaped house with a central courtyard at the front accepts the flow of qi more readily than one with a courtyard at the back.

Inauspicious – too large a door may mean a loss of beneficial energy

Inauspicious – too small a door may mean a constriction of beneficial energy

Auspicious – door proportional to the house

YOUR FRONT DOOR

The front door is one of the most important areas of your home in feng shui terms because it is the main entrance point for qi. It is important that your front door is facing the most auspicious direction for you (see pages 22–27) and that it is the recipient of a gentle flow of positive qi. This can be created by making a garden path that curves to your door.

It is particularly important that your front door is not obstructed or not receiving negative energy or sha qi. Otherwise known as the "killing breath" or "poison arrows", sha qi can be created in a number of different ways. The flow of sha qi can be produced by sharp angles being aimed at your house, for example, by the sharp angle of a neighbor's roofline or the positioning of a tower or a pole directly opposite the center of your front door. You can deflect this negative energy by placing a bagua mirror or an ordinary mirror above your door. A bagua mirror is an octagonal disk with a small convex mirror in the center surrounded by the eight auspicious trigrams (see pages 20–21).

Sha qi also travels along straight lines — a road or an avenue of trees can lead sha qi to your front door. You can plant a hedge to deflect it.

Feng Shui Tip

Make sure that your front door is in proportion to your house and the size of an average person. An entrance that is too large could lead to loss of money while a front door that is too small may constrict the flow of beneficial energy into the house, leaving the occupants feeling impoverished.

It is important that the rooms of your house are a regular shape and that you use symmetry in your style of decoration. Particular problems occur in L-shaped rooms or rooms that have a prominent corner. This causes a poison arrow to pierce the interior, which needs to be negated.

You can do this by hanging a wind chime in front of the corner or by placing a leafy potted plant or a crystal in front of the corner's angle. Imagine the angle made by the corner as the head of the arrow. Trace the line of the arrow across the room to where it hits the opposite wall. It would also be a good idea to also place a potted plant in that position.

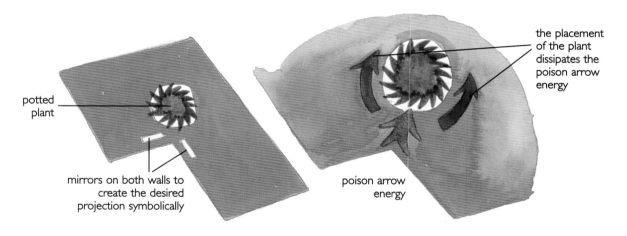

potted plant

mirrors on both walls to create the desired projection symbolically

the placement of the plant dissipates the poison arrow energy

poison arrow energy

For good feng shui, make sure that the pieces of furniture you use are in proportion with the space and ceiling height of the room (see also page 69). Overly large pieces of furniture may introduce a more aggressive, yang energy than the room can balance with yin space. Also use furniture that echoes the shape of the room — for instance, two rectangular sofas for a rectangular living room, rather than one rectangular sofa and two square wing chairs. Avoid cluttering the space — for a discussion of the harmful effects of clutter, see page 17.

Feng shui beliefs center on the balance of yin and yang and the balance between the elements. The house is always related to the element of earth and is surrounded by the elements of fire, water, metal and wood.

The element of water, represented by a river or roadway, should be in front of the house, which the Chinese believe should ideally face north. The element of fire should be at the back of the house in the shape of a hill, providing protection and support. The west, which relates to the element of metal, is represented by rounded hills or metal high-rise buildings while the east, relating to the element of wood, is represented by park land, forests or even skyscrapers (because the rectangle is symbolic of the wood element). The east should be more elevated than the west so that beneficial qi, either through moving traffic or the flowing of the river, will descend gently from east to west.

The four directions around the house are also symbolized by the four celestial beasts — the crimson phoenix in the south, the black turtle in the north, the white tiger in the west and the azure dragon in the east. These represent the four major divisions of the macro-constellations in Chinese astrology and form part of the Chinese belief system concerning the intermingling of heaven qi and earth qi.

Ideally, the best place to live is in the middle of a gently sloping hillside with a mountain rising at the back of the house and an unobstructed view to the plains with a meandering river in front. Living on top of a hill can leave you feeling unprotected and vulnerable to the flow of the elements, while living at the bottom of a hill may be dangerous because the energy flowing down the mountain may create a poison arrow by the time it hits the base of the mountain. Living on a flat area, although traditionally considered inauspicious, is not considered problematic now.

Feng Shui Tip

Houses whose shape corresponds to the shape of their environment are the most stable. However, for a prosperous life, the following combinations are ideal:

☯ a house made of concrete and bricks (earth) is best suited to mountainous terrain (fire);

☯ a house with a corrugated roof or a large-scale metal skyscraper (metal) is best situated near large bodies of water (water);

☯ a house of irregular shapes and sizes (water) is best suited to a rounded hillside or large-scale metal buildings (metal);

☯ a house with wooden cladding or an apartment block (wood) is best situated near large bodies of water (water); and

☯ a house with a sharp roofline (fire) is best situated near a forest or skyscrapers (wood).

THE ROAD OUTSIDE YOUR DOOR

In feng shui, the movement of water in a river is now equated with the flow of traffic along the road outside your front door. Traditionally, it was believed that living in an area where the streets all run parallel to each other in a grid formation caused bad feng shui, but now only busy thoroughfares are believed to be particularly bad feng shui.

auspicious

Straight streets that do not have too much traffic are not considered a problem unless your house is situated at a T-intersection, at the end of a dead end street or on the apex of a sharp bend. It is best to avoid houses that have such strong energy flowing directly at the house.

inauspicious

However, it is possible to deflect the worst of the energy by planting a hedge or constructing a fence. The energy flowing along a roadway is too strong and is no longer beneficial, becoming a poison arrow of negative energy. Living on the corner of a street is also inauspicious, mainly because the energy flowing past the front of your house is dispersed by the energy flowing past your house on either side.

The ideal position is a meandering roadway or path that leads past your front door in a gentle curve. Living in a cul-de-sac is also auspicious.

auspicious

inauspicious

inauspicious

inauspicious

inauspicious

34

In feng shui, it is considered prudent to avoid living near areas or buildings that have a poor balance of yin and yang energy. Schools traditionally have an excess of yang energy and can cause people living near them to feel a low-level sense of unease.

Students living near their college or university should take care to go away for breaks between semesters to recover fully from being exposed to very strong yang energy. This is less necessary if the buildings of the college or university are not densely packed and are balanced with large expanses of grass and trees. Similarly, living near power lines, airports or areas which attract a lot of human traffic, such as rail stations and factories, should be avoided.

Places that are excessively yin in energy are characterized by an association with death, grieving and feelings of distress. It is best to avoid living near churches, graveyards and police stations. It is also important to find out whether the previous owners of your house suffered mental illnesses, divorce or untimely death while living in the house. Be wary if the house is being sold as part of a divorce settlement.

Sewerage installations and garbage dumps create a stagnant energy that causes negative energy to pervade your home. Since the practice of extending shorelines or filling in undesirably shaped terrain with landfill is common, check that your new house, apartment or townhouse was not built upon reclaimed terrain.

A Checklist for the Ideal Home

If you are in the enviable position of starting afresh and want to use feng shui to choose your new house, consider the following checklist as a summary of some of the most important questions you should ask yourself when deciding on your house. This checklist will help you narrow down your choices. At that stage, think carefully about the house or houses left on the list and see if your intuition can tell you something about the energy flow of the property. If you feel too close to the issue, consider bringing in a feng shui practitioner to help you with your final decision.

The checklist has been devised in the form of questions to which you can respond either yes or no and page references that will help you make each decision. Place a tick in either the "yes" or "no" column. Add up the yes and no responses. The house which has inspired no more than three negative responses should be placed on your list of possible homes.

Questions	Yes	No	Page reference
LOCATION			
1. Is the street reasonably quiet and free from heavy traffic?			Page 34
2. Does a road run past the house?			Page 34
3. Is there a hill or bank of trees at the back of the property?			Pages 32–33
4. Is the front of the property free from obstruction (pole, factory or other large building)?			Page 30
5. Is the property near a lake or parkland?			Pages 32–33
6. Is the property situated away from power lines?			Page 35
7. Is the property situated away from a school (outside a one-mile radius)?			Page 35

Questions	Yes	No	Page reference
8. Is the property situated away from a graveyard (not in view of the house?)			Page 35
9. Is the property built on land other than a landfill or garbage dump?			Page 35
10. Is the property situated away from a church or funeral home (outside a one-mile radius?)			Page 35
11. Have the previous occupants been free from physical or emotional illness and divorce?			Page 35
12. Is the house free from a history of upheaval or violence?			Page 35
THE PROPERTY			
1. Does the plot of land have a regular shape?			Pages 28–29
2. Is the house regularly shaped?			Pages 28–29
3. Is the house situated either in the middle or towards the front of the plot of land with a good-sized front yard?			Pages 28–29
4. Is the front door of the right proportions for a person of average size?			Page 30
5. Are the rooms regular in size?			Page 31
6. Is the front door situated in a northerly direction?			
EAST/WEST ORIENTATION			
1. Does the front door face any of your lucky directions?			Pages 22–23
2. Does the position of the house correspond with your east/west orientation?			Pages 22–25
3. Does the bedroom allow you to place your bed in your lucky direction?			Pages 26–27
4. Does the room of your potential home office allow you to place your desk in your lucky direction?			Pages 26–27

Feng Shui Cures

WHAT ARE FENG SHUI CURES?

I f there is a poor flow of qi within a building, sometimes the removal of old walls, the construction of new walls or the blocking or installation of a window is required to allow the proper flow of qi. Sometimes, the entrance door will need to be changed so that it faces a different direction or built-in wardrobes will need to be taken out so that a bed can be placed facing the right direction for its occupant.

What if you cannot afford to do any of those things or the reconstruction of part of the building is not practicable? Would you need to vacate the premises? Although there are some imbalances that cannot be rectified, such as living under or close to power lines (see page 35), quite a number of remedies can be used to add balance to your home and your life.

These remedies symbolize the balancing of forms and elements, or yin and yang energies, to correct the flow. They will be discussed on the following pages:

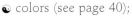

- colors (see page 40);
- lights and mirrors (see page 41);
- metal chimes and bells (see page 42);
- plants and pets (see page 43);
- mobiles and flags (see page 44);
- solid objects, statues and rocks (see page 45);
- fans and flutes (see page 46); and
- music (see page 47).

These cures can be used to block harmful energy, slow down the flow of energy and enhance the benefit in a particular area of the building.

For issues concerning the energy around electrical equipment, see page 47. To use your intuition to choose an appropriate feng shui cure, see page 39.

There are many people who instinctively know about the flow of energy in their house or place of business and who follow their intuition unconsciously, understanding how to make the most of their environment. Often the homes of these types of people are comfortable and a joy to visit.

Many of us, to some degree or other, have a feeling about what would look good in a particular room, although we don't know why. The placement of a potted palm in a certain corner may be satisfying to us, without our realizing that the plant now shields us from a poison arrow created by a protruding corner. It is important to follow your intuition about the way your home feels. Your feelings may also be in tune with the seasonal variations of light and warmth, making you want to put warm yang colors in a southeast room which is decorated in forest greens. It is sensible to follow such instincts.

At times, though, there may be some areas that just don't work, no matter what you try. This is where feng shui becomes particularly useful, by helping you identify where the qi is stagnating and choosing the feng shui solution that will encourage the qi to flow harmoniously through the area.

It is also beneficial to use your intuition when deciding how many feng shui cures you are going to use at once. Make the most appropriate changes and allow a period of time to elapse to see if you can sense any subtle changes in the way the affected area feels. Make sure that you only try a few cures at a time, as too many cures may become clutter in themselves.

tranquility - *an*

COLORS

Colors, like shapes, directions and aspirations, correspond with the Chinese elements of wood, water, earth, fire and metal. The following table lists the correspondences between elements, colors, directions and the type of energy the color generates:

Element	Color	Direction	Yin/Yang
Earth	Yellow	Center	Yang
Water	Black	North	Yin
Fire	Red	South	Yang
Wood	Blue/green	East	Yin
Metal	White	West	Yang

To stimulate qi energy in your home or office, it is a good idea to use bright yang colors, such as reds and yellows. The use of strong colors, such as red, black and gold (a richer version of yellow) invites good prosperity into the building. However, too much yang energy may be detrimental. It is important to achieve a balance between yin and yang colors (see pages 10–11).

If you are unsure about incorporating a particular color into a certain room, get a swatch of the color and leave it in the room for a few days. See if the color makes any difference to the energy of the room. For strong imbalances, you may wish to change the color of the walls, but often all that is needed is a couple of cushions or candles in the right color to help balance the energy of the room.

Consider using color remedies for stimulating the creativity/children aspiration area of your house or place of business (see pages 18–21).

LIGHTS AND MIRRORS

Lights, mirrors, crystals and other reflective surfaces are excellent for deflecting poison arrows of negative energy and bringing yang qualities to balance a dark, overly yin room. Any feelings of depression or unease in a room can be lifted by putting candles or floor lamps that spread their light upward to the corners of the room. Always make sure that these cures come in pairs or in even-numbered sets, for instance, four or six candles. Also make sure that the lamps do not have too many sharp angles.

Having a light permanently on near your front door will help deflect any negative energy projected by an oncoming roadway, power pole or tower. You may also wish to use a mirror above your front door to keep it clear of any negative qi. Although a flat mirror will work, it is best to use a convex mirror to diffuse the negative energy more efficiently. A light or flagpole may be incorporated in your garden to balance any irregular shaping of your house and give it a sense of symmetry.

Mirrors can be positioned on your walls so that they reflect a pleasant aspect, preferably from outside your house. It is important not to allow two mirrors to be positioned on opposite walls so that they reflect each other.

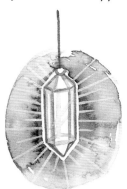

Crystals are also useful in diffusing negative energies and encouraging strong positive qi to stimulate the energy of a room. Crystal chandeliers with evenly faceted glass crystals are desirable in large rooms. In smaller rooms, place a crystal in the window to enliven the room's energy.

Consider using lights, mirrors and crystals for stimulating the fame and acknowledgment aspiration area of your house or place of business (see pages 18–21).

CHIMES AND BELLS

Wind chimes and bells help activate stagnant energy in a building. Corners are particularly notorious for the build-up of stagnant negative energy. This can be dispersed by clapping or ringing a melodious bell in each corner of each room of the building. This is a good practice to include in your spring cleaning routine.

Wind chimes are also excellent for slowing down energy that is rushing along a straight corridor or flight of stairs. If the front door is positioned in view of the back door, this encourages the fast passage of qi energy through the house, and does not allow the energy to move beneficially throughout the building. Wind chimes placed near the front door will help slow down the energy, encouraging it to move into different areas of the house, rather than out the back door.

Choose wind chimes that sound melodious to your ears, as chimes, whether they are made of metal, wood or bamboo, can attract prosperous energy into the building. The sound of moving water also enhances beneficial energy.

Consider using chimes and bells for stimulating the mentors and travel aspiration area of your house or place of business (see pages 18–21).

PLANTS AND PETS

Living plants and animals are used as cures to stimulate energy in a home or place of business. Potted
plants are particularly useful for deflecting poison
arrow energy from protruding corners or slowing
down fast-moving energy along a straight corridor.
A potted plant situated just inside a front door that is
positioned directly opposite the back door can cure the
fast passage of energy through the house.

It is important to keep your indoor plants healthy and
in contact with enough sunlight to prosper. To increase wealth
in the family consider placing a coin into the soil of
your potted plant. Popular indoor plants for prosperity include
the "money plant", otherwise known as a dracaena, an
evergreen which thrives indoors.

You may consider including indoor plants that have brightly
coloured yellow, orange or red-hued flowers. These types of plants
would be particularly beneficial near a window in dark, yin rooms.
An aquarium of brightly colored fish, such as goldfish, can also be used to
balance the yin energy of a room and enhance the flow of wealth into the house.
Animals generally are good feng shui. Pets are well known for their ability to
circulate energy around the house and are helpful in
relieving stress.

Consider using plants and keeping pets to
enhance the wealth area of your house or place
of business (see pages 18–21).

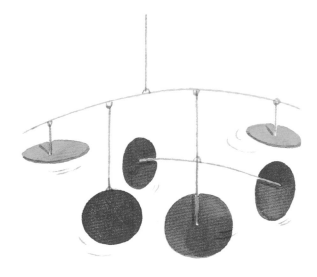

MOBILES AND FLAGS

Mobiles, whirligigs, weathervanes, flags and other flexible objects move with the flow of the wind deflect poison arrow energy and encourage beneficial energy through your home or place of business.

If your bathroom is windowless, the potential stagnation of energy in the room can be alleviated by tying a red ribbon to the ventilation grill. Stagnation of energy in the corners of a particular room can also be dissipated by placing a mobile or whirligig in the corners. These types of objects should be made of natural materials, such as handmade paper or wood.

The stagnant energy in corners can also be dissipated by burning of incense in each corner of the room. Choose an incense that contains good quality ingredients and avoid incense which contains a lot of chemicals or is based on dung.

A weathervane should be used if you can see the sharp edge of a neighboring roof line pointed towards your building. The movement of the weathervane will deflect the poison arrow energy made by the sharp angles of your neighbor's house.

Consider using mobiles and other similar remedies for stimulating the relationship area of your house or place of business (see pages 18–21).

SOLID OBJECTS, STATUES AND ROCKS

Solid, heavy objects can help slow qi that is moving too fast through a building. If the energy is accelerated by being channeled down a straight corridor, consider using a statue or large piece of furniture that does not have many sharp edges, such as a heavy wing chair, at the beginning or end of the corridor. It is important that the heavy objects you use are rounded because this will encourage the energy to slow down in order to move around the object in its path. A round-edged table placed in a long hallway will slow down the flow of energy. However, ensure that the large object is in proportion with the room; otherwise, the piece may take on a strong yang energy which will exacerbate the aggressively yang nature of the fast-moving qi moving towards or past it. If you are using a functional piece of furniture, such as a chair, make sure that you only use it for visitors or decorative purposes. The strong energy striking the chair would not be conducive to relaxation.

Consider using statues and other heavy objects for stimulating the creativity and children aspiration area of your house or place of business (see pages 18–21).

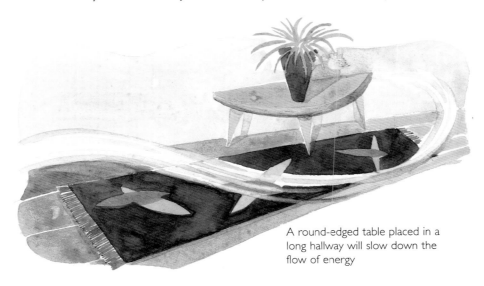

A round-edged table placed in a long hallway will slow down the flow of energy

FANS AND FLUTES

Fans and flutes are useful for dissipating poison arrow energy moving quickly along long, straight corridors and for diffusing the negative energy of an exposed beam. Overhead beams that protrude from the ceiling or are exposed create a network of poison arrow energy that can be quite harmful. It is particularly harmful to use a desk or sleep in a bed which is situated under a beam. Illnesses, ranging from mild headaches to serious diseases, can be caused by sleeping under a beam.

A popular cure for the negative energy caused by beams is to position another straight-sided object that is positioned perpendicular to the beam to diffuse its strong destructive energy; such as two bamboo flutes or wind chimes tied to the beam with red string.

Consider using fans and flutes for stimulating the family and health aspiration area of your house or place of business (see pages 18–21).

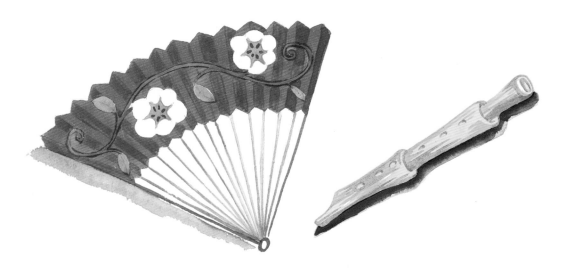

ELECTRICAL EQUIPMENT

Music from stereo systems, televisions and radios can provide an effective yang energy to counterbalance a dark, yin room. Music that can be heard through the house can stimulate stagnant qi. However, it is important that the sound is not overly loud or discordant.

Generally, you should only have electrical appliances that are necessary in your house. It is thought advisable that the yang energy generated by electrical appliances should be masked when not in use. Television and stereo cabinets, as well as home office cabinets that can house computer equipment, should be considered. If you cannot get this type of furniture, you can use a dark cloth to cover the appliance and neutralize the potentially harmful yang energy. Electrical appliances should not be used in the bedroom because of their potential to disrupt sleep patterns.

Consider using your stereo system and other sound equipment for stimulating the knowledge aspiration area of your house or place of business (see pages 18–21).

ambition - *chih*

Wealth, Acknowledgment and Fame

THE WEALTH AREA

To enhance the flow of beneficial qi in the area of your house or place of business that resonates with wealth qi, you will first need to identify your wealth area (see pages 18–21) and then use auspicious symbols to attract wealth into your life. Gold and both manufactured and naturally occurring gold objects, such as oranges and pineapples, are considered symbols of good luck.

According to the ancient Chinese beliefs system, there are three types of luck. As well as fate and the luck that you create for yourself, there is also a form of luck which encompasses feng shui, called "Earth Luck". This type of luck is created when you are attuned with the energy of the earth using feng shui principles, and it helps you mitigate even the worst of fates.

The placement of good luck or wealth symbols in the home is important. Never place them on the floor or in a low position. These symbols need to be placed in an elevated location, such as on a mantelpiece or above the door.

ATTRACTING WEALTH ENERGY TO YOUR DOOR

When decorating your wealth area, keep in mind that this area resonates with the element of wood and allow this to influence the color schemes and objects you use to decorate this part of the house. Light greens and shades of brown and tan will enhance the wealth energy in your home, as will incorporating potted plants. One simple way to increase your wealth is to place three gold-colored coins that have been wrapped in red paper under a potted plant.

Metal is harmful to wood, so do not use much metal; concentrating on water and wood motifs. You may even consider installing an aquarium with nine fish, preferably eight goldfish and one black fish. The symbolic role of the black fish is to attract and destroy bad wealth energy that strays into your home.

Attracting wealth energy to your door

If you are building a new house or repaving your driveway, consider burying six coins in your driveway before you lay the cement, gravel or paving stones. Bury the coins along a imaginary line that leads to your entrance, as this will attract abundant wealth energy to your door. Alternatively, place nine coins under your welcome mat.

Lucky or favorable numbers can be worked out according to the formulas outlined on pages 22–23. In feng shui, certain numbers attract good or bad luck. For example, the number 4 is believed to be bad luck, auguring death, while 5 is thought to be a lucky number because it symbolizes the five elements — earth, water, fire, wood and metal — which form the basis of Chinese medicine and religious beliefs.

Chinese Good Luck Numbers

2 - easy fulfilment
5 - good luck
6 - wealth
8 - good business, wealth
9 - recognition, completion
10 - confidence

Using the luo-shu square, you can use your lucky numbers to work out which areas are favorable to you. However, what if the area that corresponds with the wealth qi is in a direction unfavorable to you?

Work out your lucky number and the directions that are favorable to you. If the wealth area is not in a favorable direction, you can balance the wealth area in your favor. This can be done by placing a bowl of water in the wealth area. Remember to change the water every few days.

How to Avoid Flushing Your Money Away

If your house or place of business is an irregular shape and the particular corner that resonates with wealth qi is missing, you will continually have problems with your finances. The cure is to square off that portion of the building and make it appear to be a regular shape. To square off, continue the lines of the two walls that would make up that corner and find the point in the garden where they meet. To emphasize this projected corner, feng shui practitioners often advise including a water fountain or other water feature. To highlight the wealth-enhancing factor, you may wish to make a kidney-shaped pond and have a few goldfish or, if there is enough room, some carp, swimming in it.

If your wealth corner contains one of the house's water features, such as a bathroom, toilet, kitchen or laundry, be careful that you are not flushing away your wealth energy. Wealth is particularly linked with yin energy and the element of water. It follows that all areas in your home dealing with water, such as sinks, bath and laundry tubs and toilets, must be in good working order and not blocked in any way.

So that you are not losing your wealth, it is important to do the following things:

- fix leaky taps immediately;

- always flush your toilet with the lid down;

- cover all floor drain holes and sink holes; and

- keep the laundry, toilet and bathroom doors closed at all times.

ACKNOWLEDGMENT AND FAME AREA

The acknowledgment and fame area corresponds with the element of fire and its energy can be enhanced by placing items in it that are predominantly wood- or plant-related. Try to avoid having any water features in this area. If you have a kitchen, bathroom or toilet in this area, hang a mirror outside the door to that room. If these rooms are dark, add light by means of an extra mirror, large candles or a ventilated skylight.

If you have an entrance in this area, make sure your entrance hall is light and uncluttered to encourage the entry of beneficial qi. If the hallway is dark, consider a skylight. Place a doormat outside your entrance door and make sure that it incorporates the word "Welcome" and that its color scheme includes red, maroon or orange.

If your acknowledgment and fame area is not an interior but a courtyard bounded by the walls of the building on both sides, consider installing solar-powered garden lights. If your courtyard is densely planted, be careful to keep it well-pruned to let more light in. Timber frames or wooden gates can be backed with mirrors and attached to the walls to add interest and increase the flow of qi. Include wooden garden furniture and stain it to enhance its own natural color or choose a reddish, mahogany stain to activate the fire element in the acknowledgment and fame area. If you wish to paint your furniture, choose colors that correspond with element of fire.

To avoid stagnation in the corners of the courtyard and to deflect any poison arrows, place tubs of planted trees, climbers, flowers or kitchen herbs in the corners. Choose plants, both for the interior and exterior, that do not need pruning or that will not be allowed to spread naturally. Select flowers or plants that are strongly scented or tall with sharp points, such as foxgloves or irises. It is important not to neglect this area and to keep it clean, well-tended and clear of debris.

To identify the acknowledgment and fame area, see pages 18–27.

ATTRACTING ACKNOWLEDGMENT

If you work at a desk or other tabletop, you can use feng shui to increase your sense of acknowledgment. The first step is to move your desk into an auspicious position, placed so that you are facing the wall which frames the doorway leading into your office. Sitting with your back to a door will lead you to your being overlooked for promotion and can even make you vulnerable to retrenchment or demotion.

If possible, position your tabletop so that it faces one of your favorable directions (see pages 22–23). Generally, it is thought favorable to sit facing the south or south-east direction to attract wealth and acknowledgment qi.

However, often you are not able to move your office furniture to allow for feng shui. If this is so and your back is facing the entrance to your office, you can cure this bad qi energy by placing a mirror on your tabletop so that the entrance is reflected in it.

Good luck and fortune can be encouraged by the state of your tabletop. Above all else, your desk must be absolutely clear of clutter. Remove all objects that are not in everyday use and keep your desk drawers tidy and functional. This in itself will attract good feng shui.

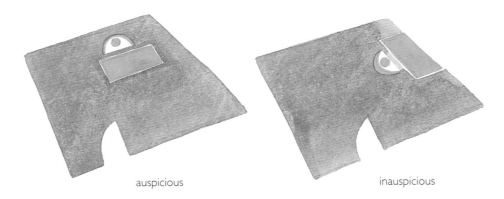

auspicious   inauspicious

If you sit at a desk or use a tabletop to do business with your customers, you may enhance any of the eight aspirations (see pages 14–15) by mentally subdividing the tabletop into the following nine sections and placing good luck symbols in strategic places.

fame

The middle top-third section of your tabletop corresponds with the acknowledgment and fame area. To encourage good fortune in this area, place a picture of brightly colored flowers or a package of three coins wrapped in red paper or tied up with red ribbon or thread in the area. Depending on your aesthetic preference, you may wish to use a small artificial jade tree or some brightly colored silk or wooden carved flowers instead. If you prefer living plants, do not use those that are stunted in their growth or prickly to touch, such as bonsai trees, shrubs, roses or cactuses.

Feng Shui Tip

Make sure that your desk or tabletop is in proportion to the room and that it is not creating a yang energy that is too strong. You may find that you suffer a number of headaches in the office if your desk is too big for your space or its color is too strong, such as black.

Lovers, Mentors and Family

THE RELATIONSHIP AREA

Check the colors and lighting used in your relationship area. Be careful to include a balance of cool and warm colors, and make sure there is a balance between furniture and space. Include bright, warmly colored throw rugs or cushions if you are in the courting stages of your relationship or if you wish to revitalize the romance in your life. Place crystals, particularly rose quartz, in the area or more candles to increase light.

Try to have a pair of objects, pictures or furniture for balance and as a symbol of the type of energy you wish for your life. For example, have two candles, two complementary pictures or paintings, or two armchairs arranged symmetrically. Do the same in your bedroom. You may include symbols of conjugal happiness, such as two entwined hearts, two ducks or a picture of a peony.

In both your bedroom and the relationships area, display photographs of yourself and your partner or of happy couples. Make sure that they do not clutter the area. Keep this area clean. You may also wish to add a mobile or wind chime to help move any stagnant energy in this space. The burning of incense will also stimulate beneficial qi. Choose patchouli, musk, ylang ylang or jasmine incense to generate a loving atmosphere.

The relationships area is usually in one corner of your house. If your house is an irregular shape, square off the shape and see whether there is an empty space in part or all of the relationships area. To bring beneficial qi into this area of your house and your life, plant a fruiting tree (or use a potted one) on the missing corner to strengthen that area. An alternative is to plant a love garden, incorporating flowers and herbs traditionally associated with encouraging love, such as geranium, lavender and lovage, in the missing section of the house.

If you cannot balance the corner from the outside, you can still balance it from the inside. If there are windows in the walls closest to the missing corner, hang a crystal in each window. If these walls create a protruding corner, prevent the corner from creating poison arrow energy by placing a mirror on each side of the corner to create an illusion of an outward pointing corner.

To identify your relationship area, see pages 18–21.

There are two ways of checking compatibility with your partner, friends or family. The first method is to identify yourself with one of the five elements. Follow the table on page 13 to work out which element you are. The table below shows which elements complement each other and which don't.

Your element	Compatible elements	Incompatible elements
Earth	Earth, Fire, Metal	Wood, Water
Metal	Metal, Earth, Water	Wood, Fire
Water	Water, Metal, Wood	Fire, Earth
Wood	Wood, Water, Fire	Earth, Metal
Fire	Fire, Earth, Wood	Metal, Water

There are five elemental combinations that experience difficulties in a relationship. However, if you are in this situation, you can offset some of the negative effects of the combination by infusing your relationship with goodwill and including a balancing element in your relationship area or the bedroom. If feelings are particularly fraught, consider giving your partner a present incorporating the balancing elements, as outlined below:

Difficult combinations	Balancing element	Suggestions and gift ideas
Earth and water	Metal	Metal sculpture Jewelry
Metal and wood	Water	Aquarium Weekend at a beach resort
Water and fire	Wood	Large potted plants Wicker picnic basket
Wood and earth	Fire	Good-quality incense Romantic scented candles
Fire and metal	Earth	Large blue and white earthenware jars or tubs Blue and white cups or plates

The second method of ascertaining your compatibility with others is to determine whether you and your partner have an east or west orientation. Look at pages 22–23 to see how to work out whether you have an east or west group of numbers and favorable directions. From a feng shui perspective, it is strongly advised that for a long-lasting and harmonious relationship, the people are within the same group. This is recommended for married couples, as well as for relationships between parents and children.

Make a note of the number which you obtained using the formulas on pages 22–23. Follow the table below to find out which is your auspicious relationship direction. To bring greater luck in finding your true love, sleep with your head pointing in your auspicious relationship direction.

Personal number	Auspicious direction for a male	Auspicious direction for a female
1	South	South
2	North-west	North-west
3	South-east	South-east
4	East	East
5	North-west	West
6	South-west	South-west
7	North-east	North-east
8	West	West
9	North	North

To enhance the flow of beneficial qi in the area of your house or place of business that corresponds with beneficial patronage and travel, see pages 18–21 to identify where your mentor area lies.

This area is usually found in one of the corner sections of your home. If your building is an irregular shape and part or all of the mentor area is missing, follow some of the suggestions on pages 56–57. If you would like to increase your chances of meeting more helpful people or travelling, include wind chimes in that section of your home. You may also include your stereo system somewhere in the room. Do not play the music too loudly, as harsh sounds tend to disrupt the flow of beneficial qi. Apart from traditional feng shui cures, you can also do good deeds for others to help kick-start the flow of energy in this area.

To activate this aspiration further, circulate more light through the area by using crystals, any type of glass ornament or a mirror which reflects a pleasant aspect of the room or a pretty view outside your building. Incorporate photographs or paintings featuring a group of people enjoying each other's company.

destiny - *ming*

Another way of activating a particular area of your home or place or business is to incorporate something that resonates with your personal element. To find out what your element is, see page 13. The table below provides some suggestions as to some types of objects you could include in your mentor area to enhance your good fortune.

Your element	Suggestions
Earth	A brown ceramic cup
Metal	Metal wind chimes
Wood	A drawing or a picture on paper of a powerful person
Water	Clear bowl with colorful marbles or glass chips filled with water with a lighted floating candle
Fire	Red or orange candle

If your windows in this area face a gloomy aspect or an unattractive view, such as a brick wall, use attractive drapes, preferably with swags and a generous amount of material, to balance the yin nature of the windows. For the mentor area, try to incorporate some yellow or gold into the color scheme of the curtains or use colorful tassels to hold the curtains back from the window. Also, keeping the window curtains open during the evening is bad feng shui.

THE FAMILY AREA

To enhance the flow of beneficial qi in the area of your house that corresponds with a harmonious family, turn to pages 18–21 to identify your family area. To bring greater harmony to the family, place a brightly colored fan or a flute decorated with bright green and yellow ribbons somewhere in the interior, as well as checking for imbalances between yin and yang energy (see pages 10–11) and areas of clutter that require tidying. Also, place photographs and paintings of your family members or ancestors in this area.

Communication is one of the most important considerations when dealing with relationship issues in marriage, friendships or within your family. Make sure that the doors leading into the family area are all in good working order as they are symbolic of strong communication of qi between the rooms.

If the doors stick or are otherwise in disrepair, tension will mount within the house. In feng shui, the front and back doors must not face each other, nor should three doorways be aligned along a corridor. Place a screen near the back door, shielding the door from sight of the front door. If there is a doorway between the front and back doors, place a beaded or lace curtain or a wind chime in the doorway.

The family area also corresponds with your health and that of your family. The bathroom will often be located in this area (see page 75).

harmony - *ho*

It is important to take note of the lucky direction of each member of your family (see pages 22–23). Living in a house that resonates for only some members of the family can cause enormous difficulties and clashes. Also check the elemental orientation between family members and the solutions for those members who are not elementally compatible (see pages 58–59).

If a member of your family or workforce is feeling particularly hostile, there are two important aspects that can be changed that may help make that person feel more comfortable. First, check whether their entrance into the building should be changed. Ideally, it should be suited to their favorable number (see pages 22–23). See the table on page 59 to work out the best direction for a person's entrance.

Secondly, ensure that the person is sleeping with their head pointing in their favorable direction and that they are working at their desk or workstation facing their favorable direction. If that direction is not available, choose one of the other three directions that suit with the person's orientation group (see pages 22–23).

A significant rearrangement of the house or office might be needed to make these changes. The benefits, however, can be great.

Feng Shui Tip

Do not store objects or clutter under your bed as you are likely to have disturbed rest — you are, in fact, sleeping on problems.

Career, Knowledge and Creativity

THE CAREER AREA

The career area is usually situated between two corners of your building. If this area is missing because you have a recessed entrance or a courtyard at the sides or back of the building, you may wish to make a feature of it, which will make the shape of the building regular (see pages 52–53 for further decorating ideas).

This area corresponds with the element of water, and its energy can be enhanced by placing items in it that are predominantly water-related, such as a small wall fountain, or that resonate with the energy of metal, such as decorative brass pots or photographs in silver frames. In the productive cycle of elements, metal sustains water in the same way as a metal bowl holds water, giving it form.

Try not to have any earth features in this area, such as potted plants or ceramic plates. If this area is too yin (too dark), include a brightly colored cushion or increase the level of light in the area. Always keep light fittings in good order and change light bulbs as soon as they burnt out. Always keep light bulbs covered with lamp shades or other fittings, such as Chinese rice paper lanterns.

See pages 18–21 to help you locate the career area in your house or place of business.

inauspicious

auspicious

A good way of improving your work life is to decorate your work area as harmoniously as possible and to ensure that you are not facing any blank walls in the office or work area. If you are in an open-plan office, it is best if you are sitting in a position (preferably in the southeast) where you do not have to see the backs of your colleagues. If you work at a computer, it is a good idea to take a break near a fountain or other water feature, inside or outside the building, to avoid the build-up of tension.

Look at your desk, workstation, bench or countertop. Are there any areas that are cluttered or corners that have been gathering dust? Keep your desk free of dust as a symbol of keeping your life free of stagnation. See if you can reorganize the clutter. Do not be tempted to push the clutter out of sight into cupboards or drawers, as this will make the stagnation of the beneficial qi continue.

If you are able to tap into the gentle flow of qi by organizing your work and work area so that the energy flows to you at an easy, graceful pace, you will find a corresponding benefit in your work life. You might begin to notice that panic and last-minute deadlines disappear and work begins to flow at a steady and manageable pace, allowing you to do your best and gather recognition and other rewards. See also pages 52–55 for other ways to enhance your work life.

keep your desk and drawers tidy and free of clutter to allow the gentle flow of qi

THE KNOWLEDGE AREA

The knowledge area is usually in one of the four main corners of your building. If this area is missing because your building is an irregular shape, you may wish to place an external feature where the two walls of that corner would meet if the building was a regular shape. If you are unable to make external changes, you may wish to place wind chimes in front of the corner if it is protruding into the room and producing poison arrow energy.

This corresponds with the element of wood and its energy can be enhanced by placing plants, wooden furniture and your books into it. If possible, try not to have open bookshelves, as the horizontal lines of the shelving create poison arrows. This would be a good area to store useful information in filing cabinets.

If you own a computer, this is an excellent position for it. Mechanical devices are very effective for stimultating qi in the knowledge area. Also include water elements, even if they are symbolic, such as a picture of a beautiful lake. In the productive cycle of elements, water nourishes wood. Try not to have any metal features in this area. Make sure that any frames in this area are made of wood and are not even covered with metallic paint or silver or gold leaf.

To find your knowledge area, see pages 18–21.

Feng Shui Tip

If you are a student or have a child studying at school, find the knowledge area in their bedroom and place the study desk in that part of the room. For those who work at home, it is advisable to keep the work desk and bedroom area separate.

Those who practice feng shui believe that the elements can help us understand ourselves. To do so, you need to find out what your dominant element is. The last digit of your year of birth indicates the element that dominates our personality (see pages 12–13). Each element type has distinct personality traits. A further dimension is added if you take into account whether you are the yang or yin aspect of the element.

If you are the yang aspect of an element, then you find that you strongly embody that element's characteristics. You can be more assertive and energetic. Yang energy is outgoing, active and positive. Yin energy is soft and fluid.

If you are more yin, you will have quite a few of the element's characteristics but you might also have characteristics of some of the other elements, particularly from the supporting element and also from the destructive element. For instance, if you are a yin water element, you may also have characteristics of the supportive metal element and the unsympathetic earth element (see pages 12–13 for the element diagram). The following table gives you some of the characteristics associated with each element.

Element	Personal characteristics
Earth	Loyal, attentive, thorough
	Stubborn, needy
Metal	Controlled, organized, idealistic
	Authoritative
Water	Resourceful, independent, imaginative
	Secretive, uncommunicative
Wood	Practical, open, motivated
	Competitive, restless
Fire	Compassionate, communicative, intuitive
	Willful, not focused on detail

wisdom - *chih*

THE CREATIVITY AREA

The creativity area is situated between two corners of your building. If this area is missing, either fully or partially, because you have a recessed entrance or a courtyard at the sides or back of the building, you can make a feature of the recess to make the building shape regular (see pages 52–53 for some ideas).

This area corresponds with the element of metal and its energy can be enhanced by placing items that are metallic or related to metal, such as metal wind chimes, lucky coins or a string of bells in the west side of the room. Also include objects related to the earth element, such as a display of your favorite decorative plates or a collection of brown semi-precious stones, such as ironstone, tiger eye or jasper. In the productive cycle of elements, earth is the natural home of metal. It is important not to have any fire features in this area, such as a fireplace or candles.

To find your creativity area, see pages 18–21.

THE RIGHT PROPORTIONS

Furniture, the front door, windows and other internal features must be in correct proportion with the room or wall that they occupy. If a piece of furniture is too large for the room it is in, it could create an imbalance between the flow of yin and yang energy. Consequently, by sitting in the room for a long period of time, you may start experiencing a feeling of restlessness or disquiet.

In feng shui, a door or piece of furniture is measured with a feng shui ruler. The ruler is divided into approximately 13 mm or half-inch segments. The divisions all have meanings and are grouped in fours, measuring approximately 54 mm or 2⅛ in. The full cycle is approximately 432 mm or 17 in. The table below outlines which of these divisions are auspicious. Measure your windows, door frames, furniture or the room itself to work out whether the dimensions of the objects are causing you bad luck. When measuring larger pieces, please keep in mind that the cycle of 432 mm repeats itself.

Measurement	Auspicious or inauspicious
0–2⅛ in 0–54 mm	Auspicious Money and abundance
2⅛–4 in 54–108 mm	Inauspicious Bad luck, legal difficulties and death in the family
4 in–6⅜ in 108–162 mm	Inauspicious Bad luck, theft and loss of money
6⅜–8 in 162–215 mm	Auspicious Successful children and helpful people
8–10⅝ in 215–270 mm	Auspicious Honor and reward
10 ⅝–12 in 270–324 mm	Inauspicious Loss and disgrace
12–14⅞ in 324–375 mm	Inauspicious Disease and scandal
14⅞–17 in 375–432 mm	Auspicious Abundance

Feng Shui Tip

An auspicious set of dimensions for a work desk or table is between 57⅜–59 in (146.5–151 cm) wide × 31–34 in (81–87cm) deep × 31–34 in (80–87cm) high. The measurement of 57⅜–59 in (147–151cm) attracts success from your creative projects (a successful son) and 31–34 in (81–87cm) attracts good luck in examinations.

Other lucky dimensions for larger pieces of furniture include:

- 40⅜–42 in (103–108.5cm) — added income from unexpected sources;
- 51–53⅛ in (130–135.5cm) — abundant good fortune; and
- 59–61⅝ in (151.5–156.5cm) — prosperity and recognition.

The Feng Shui Lifestyle

The following checklist has been designed to help remind you of the ways in which beneficial qi can be encouraged to flow around a room. Remember that qi must be allowed to flow freely and gently through your house or place of business. Avoid straight lines, furniture with sharp angles and exposed protruding corners. Try not to force the energy — take some time to feel how the energy flows in your building and how the flow could be improved. Use your intuition as well as the summary of feng shui guidelines in the table below.

Imbalance	Symptoms	Cures	Ref. Pages
Too much yin	Dark room Feelings of depression	Increase light. Add splashes of strong warm colors.	10–11
Too much yang	Overcrowded room headaches	Remove some of the furniture and include some dark colors in the cushions and throw rugs. Hang wind chimes over clutter.	10–11
Too much clutter	Untidiness Feelings of inability to focus or organize.	Include a symbol of your personal element. Place wooden objects or plants in the area.	17
Wealth area feels stagnant	Poor flow of money into the house.	Avoid metal objects if relevant. Cover all sink holes and keep toilet lid down.	48–51
Acknowledgment area feels stagnant	Demotion or retrenchment.	Include a symbol of your personal element in the area. Include plants or candles. Avoid water objects. Do not sit with your back to the door.	52–55

Imbalance	Symptoms	Cures	Ref. Pages
Relationship area feels stagnant	Problems with marriage or other close relationship.	Include red objects, wooden candle holders, and a symbol of your personal element in the area. Avoid water features. Include pictures of couples or groups of two around the house. Add a symbol of your personal element to the area.	56–59
Creativity/children area feels stagnant	New opportunities are rare. Trouble with your children.	Include objects symbolizing metal or earth. Avoid fire objects. Check your back door does not open to a narrow path.	68
Helpful people/ travel area feels stagnant	Unscrupulous people are around you. A feeling of being stuck in one place	Add a symbol of your personal element to the area. Include objects symbolizing metal and earth. Avoid metal objects. Engage in a project with another person or help a person in need.	60–61
Career area feels stagnant	Lack of opportunities for advancement in career. Demoralized feeling at work.	Add a symbol of your personal element to the area. Include objects symbolizing water and metal. Avoid earth objects. Spring clean the area and remove all clutter.	64
Knowledge/ education area feels stagnant	Being overlooked because of under-qualification. Inability to pass exams successfully.	Add a symbol of your personal element to the area. Include objects symbolizing water and metal. Avoid earth objects.	66
Family/health area feels stagnant	Illnesses. Feelings of tension within the family.	Add a symbol of your personal element to the area. Include objects that symbolize wood or water. Avoid metal objects Spring clean the area and remove all clutter.	62–63

One of the most important things about the bedroom is the position of the bed. It must not be placed in front of the door leading to your bedroom. This bed position is called the "coffin position" and signifies death. If you have a master bathroom, you should not be able to see the toilet or have the bathroom mirror reflect your bed. In fact, it is inauspicious to have a mirror anywhere in your bedroom. Full-length mirrors on the doors of built-in wardrobes are considered to be particularly harmful. Feng shui practitioners believe that the resting occupant is disturbed by spirits created by the reflection of you in the mirror while you are sleeping.

The television should also be kept out of the bedroom because the strong yang energy conducted through the television, even when it is not on, it is highly disruptive to a proper, restful sleep.

A bedroom located in the relationships or family/health sector of the house is very auspicious.

bed

inauspicious mirror /TV

inauspicious mirrors on built-in closets

bed

inauspicious placement of bed

Feng Shui Tip

Don't forget to work out your favorable directions and make sure that you do not sleep with your head pointing in an inauspicious direction.

YOUR CHILD'S BEDROOM

The same rules for an adult's bedroom apply to a child's bedroom. However, in feng shui, there are some special considerations. It is equally important to keep the child's bed from being directly opposite the doorway, with the foot of the bed pointing towards the door. Choose a spot in the room where the child can see the door and where he or she feels snug and secure, possibly in a corner.

Work out your child's element and favorable direction and make sure that he or she is sleeping with his or her head pointing in the right direction. This will give the child a peaceful sleep and a feeling of being nurtured. Include objects that symbolize the child's element, as well as the supportive element. For instance, if your child is an earth element, include symbolic earth objects or colors as well as symbolic fire objects or colors. Minimize wooden objects for an earth element child (see pages 12–13).

If a child's window faces west, place a mobile or wind chime to minimize any disruptive energy from that direction (see pages 32–33) and, if possible, choose a room for your child that catches the light of the morning sun.

Feng Shui Tip

Electric blankets are not advised for children as they conduct an electrical current which can cause drowsiness and lethargy. If your child must have an electric blanket, turn it off before the child gets into bed.

YOUR LIVING ROOM

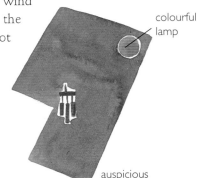

auspicious

The auspicious placement of furniture in your living room is one of the key requirements for the beneficial flow of energy. It is important that the backs of chairs and sofas are not facing the front door and that the sofa is placed, if convenient, with its back against a wall.

There is a spot in a room called "the honored guest". This is the chair in the living room or at a dining table that you first see as you enter the room. Try to have this chair facing the doorway and make sure that the view (either internally or externally) from this chair is particularly pleasant.

For the rest of the chairs and sofas in the living room, it is auspicious for the seating to be grouped in a circle or in an octagonal formation. This will create friendly conversation. Try not to allow the television or stereo to have pride of place in the living room. Instead, keep electrical equipment hidden away in a cabinet or place a dark cloth over it when not in use.

If your living room has a fireplace, keep it clean and free of ash. If the fireplace is positioned facing west, place a screen mesh in front of the hearth in winter or a decorated fire screen in summer, as the energy from the west is thought to be quite disruptive. Corner fireplaces create the best flow of qi in a living room, as the qi is directed past any corners.

Be sure to guard against poison arrow energy emanating from protruding corners in L-shaped rooms by placing a plant, some wind chimes or a mirror in front of the corner. Also make sure that the flow of qi is not stagnant in any alcoves. Stagnation can be avoided by the placement of a colorful lamp, for instance, a Tiffany-style leadlight glass lamp.

colourful lamp

auspicious

Your Bathroom

The position of your bathroom and toilet is particularly important in terms of your wealth. If the bathroom and toilet are in your wealth area, you may find that money never stays long in your household. Another inauspicious position for these rooms is if they are close to or within view of the front door. It is recommended, particularly if you are renovating and are considering putting in a second story, that you do not have your bathroom on the second floor over the entrance.

If the bathroom and toilet are inauspiciously placed, always make sure that the doors are always kept closed and that a mirror is placed over or on the outside of the doors, which symbolically negates these rooms. It is also extremely important to keep the toilet seat lid closed when not in use and have a mirror glued to the top of the lid. In feng shui, flushing the toilet with the lid up means symbolically that you are flushing away your money (see also page 51). If you are planning to build a house, do not put the toilet in the same room as the bathroom as this encourages overwhelming yin energy.

If you are worried about steam and ventilation issues, see if you can have some ventilation or fans installed in these rooms and place red ribbons or wind chimes to keep the beneficial energy moving in these areas, which are usually small and cramped. If your bathroom is too dark, bring in as much light and bright colors as possible to balance the yin darkness and yin function of the bathroom. You may consider installing a skylight, or including a bright border of tiles or new warmly colored towels to enliven the bathroom.

One of the most auspicious areas of the kitchen is the stove. The state and position of your stove is strongly linked with the state of your fortune. It is important to keep it as clean as possible, in good working order and to rotate the use of each stove element or burner. This helps move any stagnant energy concerning your finances and may even lead to a healthier bank balance. Make sure that there is nothing undermining the fire element that your stove symbolizes, such as water pipes. The element of water is particularly harmful to the fire element, as water can put out a fire. Do not have your sink right next to your oven or stove. If you do, place a (preferably wooden) divider between the two. Also, try to avoid having your oven opposite your stove.

Make sure that when you are cooking at the stove, you do not have your back to the door. The best position for the stove is in a space diagonally opposite the entrance. The best direction for the stove to face is in the south-easterly direction, which will increase your luck in business and finance.

Be careful that your kitchen cannot be seen from the front door. A kitchen in the center of the house is also inauspicious.

auspicious – the stove is separated from the sink by a divider and a mirror is placed above the stove

inauspicious – stove and sink are right next to each other

YOUR DINING ROOM

The dining room is a place where food and friendship are honored. To aid digestion, it is believed that certain feng shui principles must be observed. The first aspect to consider is the dining table. The shape of the dining table can aid a party or destroy it. Circular, oval or octagonal shapes are best. Some feng shui practitioners believe that square dining tables provoke arguments because the sharp edges of the table sends poison arrow energy around the table. If you have experienced an increase in arguments around your square table, place a circular or octagonal centerpiece on it.

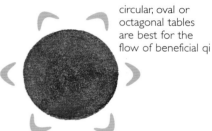

circular, oval or octagonal tables are best for the flow of beneficial qi

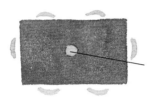

circular object to offset the corners on square/rectangular table

The table must be able to accommodate an even number of people and it is auspicious to invite an even number of guests. The chairs must be comfortable, and, if possible, offer your guests chairs with arms instead of side chairs. Chairs with arms such as carvers are symbols of the nurturing shape of the landscape that ideally surrounds your house (see pages 32–33) and symbolizes your nurturing attitude towards your guests.

If your dining room is part of the living room, try to screen off the dining area with potted plants or a wooden screen so that there are not too many distractions for your guests. It is believed that these distractions cause indigestion.

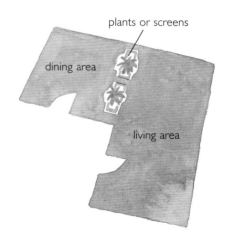

plants or screens

dining area

living area

Chinese Calendar

New year date	Element	Yin/Yang	Female (East/West)	Male (East/West)	New year date	Element	Yin/Yang	Female (East/West)	Male (East/West)
1919 Feb 1	Earth	Yin	West	East	1950 Feb 17	Metal	Yang	East	West
1920 Feb 20	Metal	Yang	West	West	1951 Feb 6	Metal	Yin	West	East
1921 Feb 8	Metal	Yin	West	West	1952 Jan 27	Water	Yang	East	East
1922 Jan 28	Water	Yang	East	West	1953 Feb 14	Water	Yin	East	West
1923 Feb 16	Water	Yin	East	West	1954 Feb 3	Wood	Yang	West	East
1924 Feb 5	Wood	Yang	West	East	1955 Jan 24	Wood	Yin	West	East
1925 Jan 24	Wood	Yin	East	East	1956 Feb 12	Fire	Yang	West	West
1926 Feb 13	Fire	Yang	East	West	1957 Jan 31	Fire	Yin	West	West
1927 Feb 2	Fire	Yin	West	East	1958 Feb 18	Earth	Yang	East	West
1928 Jan 23	Earth	Yang	West	East	1959 Feb 8	Earth	Yin	East	West
1929 Feb 10	Earth	Yin	West	West	1960 Jan 28	Metal	Yang	West	East
1930 Jan 30	Metal	Yang	West	West	1961 Feb 15	Metal	Yin	East	East
1931 Feb 17	Metal	Yin	East	West	1962 Feb 5	Water	Yang	East	West
1932 Feb 6	Water	Yang	East	West	1963 Jan 25	Water	Yin	West	East
1933 Jan 26	Water	Yin	West	East	1964 Feb 13	Wood	Yang	West	East
1934 Feb 14	Wood	Yang	East	East	1965 Feb 2	Wood	Yin	West	West
1935 Feb 4	Wood	Yin	East	West	1966 Jan 21	Fire	Yang	West	West
1936 Jan 31	Fire	Yang	West	East	1967 Feb 9	Fire	Yin	East	West
1937 Feb 11	Fire	Yin	West	East	1968 Jan 30	Earth	Yang	East	West
1938 Jan 31	Earth	Yang	West	West	1969 Feb 17	Earth	Yin	West	East
1939 Feb 19	Earth	Yin	West	West	1970 Feb 6	Metal	Yang	East	East
1940 Feb 8	Metal	Yang	East	West	1971 Jan 27	Metal	Yin	East	West
1941 Jan 27	Metal	Yin	East	West	1972 Feb 15	Water	Yang	West	East
1942 Feb 18	Water	Yang	West	East	1973 Feb 3	Water	Yin	West	East
1943 Feb 5	Water	Yin	East	East	1974 Jan 23	Wood	Yang	West	West
1944 Jan 25	Wood	Yang	East	West	1975 Feb 11	Wood	Yin	West	West
1945 Feb 13	Wood	Yin	West	East	1976 Jan 31	Fire	Yang	East	West
1946 Feb 2	Fire	Yang	West	East	1977 Feb 18	Fire	Yin	East	West
1947 Jan 22	Fire	Yin	West	West	1978 Feb 7	Earth	Yang	West	East
1948 Feb 10	Earth	Yang	West	West	1979 Jan 28	Earth	Yin	East	East
1949 Jan 29	Earth	Yin	East	West	1980 Feb 16	Metal	Yang	East	West

New year date	Element	Yin/Yang	Female (East/West)	Male (East/West)	New year date	Element	Yin/Yang	Female (East/West)	Male (East/West)
1981 Feb 5	Metal	Yin	West	East	1995 Jan 31	Wood	Yin	East	West
1982 Jan 25	Water	Yang	West	East	1996 Feb 19	Fire	Yang	West	East
1983 Feb 13	Water	Yin	West	West	1997 Feb 7	Fire	Yin	East	East
1984 Feb 2	Wood	Yang	West	West	1998 Jan 28	Earth	Yang	East	West
1985 Feb 20	Wood	Yin	East	West	1999 Feb 16	Earth	Yin	West	East
1986 Feb 9	Fire	Yang	East	West	2000 Feb 5	Metal	Yang	West	East
1987 Jan 29	Fire	Yin	West	East	2001 Jan 24	Metal	Yin	West	West
1988 Feb 17	Earth	Yang	East	East	2002 Feb 12	Water	Yang	West	West
1989 Feb 6	Earth	Yin	East	West	2003 Feb 1	Water	Yin	East	West
1990 Jan 27	Metal	Yang	West	East	2004 Jan 22	Wood	Yang	East	West
1991 Feb 15	Metal	Yin	West	East	2005 Feb 9	Wood	Yin	West	East
1992 Feb 4	Water	Yang	West	West	2006 Jan 29	Fire	Yang	East	East
1993 Jan 23	Water	Yin	West	West	2007 Feb 18	Fire	Yin	East	West
1994 Feb 10	Wood	Yang	East	West	2008 Feb 7	Earth	Yang	West	East

First published in Canada in 2000 by
Raincoast Books
8680 Cambie Street
Vancouver, B.C. V6P 6M9
(604) 323 7100
www.raincoast.com

Commissioned by Deborah Nixon
Text: Antonia Beattie and Rosemary Stevens
Designer: Sue Rawkins
Editor: Anna Bullen
Illustrations: Sue Ninham
Production Manager: Kristy Nelson
Project Co-ordinator: Clare Wallis

Canadian Cataloguing in Publication Data
Beattie, Antonia
Using Feng Shui
ISBN 1-55192-311-4
1. Feng Shui. I. Title.
BF1779.F4B42 2000   133.3'337   C99-911259-7

This book is intended to give general information only. The publishers
expressly disclaim all liability to any person arising directly or indirectly from
the use of, or for any errrors or omissions in, the information in this book.
The adoption and application of the information in this book is at the
reader's discretion and is his or her sole responsibility.

Set in Stempel Schneidler on Quark XPress
Printed in Singapore by Tien Wah Press (Pte) Ltd